W9-BCT-416

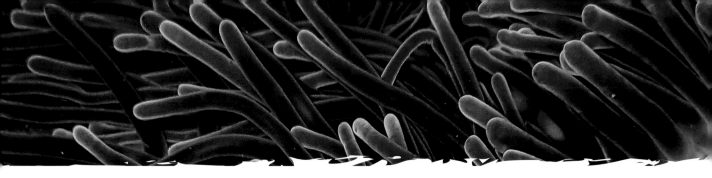

ANIMALS AT WORK

Animals
Finding Mates

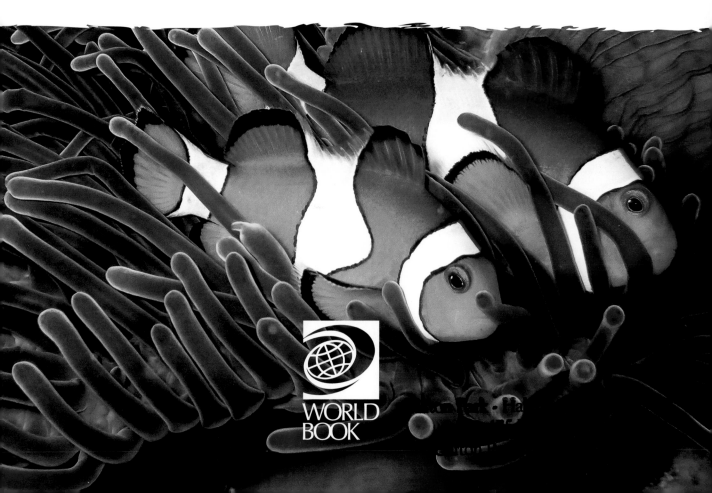

WORLD BOOK

World Book, Inc.
180 North LaSalle Street
Suite 900
Chicago, Illinois 60601
USA

Produced for World Book, Inc. by Bailey Publishing Associates Ltd.

For information about other World Book publications, visit our website at **www.worldbook.com** or call **1-800-WORLDBK (967-5325).**

Library of Congress Cataloging-in-Publication data has been applied for.

Title: Animals Finding Mates
ISBN: 978-0-7166-2731-9

Animals at Work
ISBN: 978-0-7166-2724-1 (set, hc)

Also available as:
ISBN: 978-0-7166-2744-9 (e-book)

Printed in China by Shenzhen Wing King Tong
Paper Products Co, Ltd., Shenzhen, Guangdong
1st printing August 2018

4353

Staff

Writer: Mary Auld

Executive Committee

President
Jim O'Rourke

Vice President and Editor in Chief
Paul A. Kobasa

Vice President, Finance
Donald D. Keller

Vice President, Marketing
Jean Lin

Vice President, International
Maksim Rutenberg

Vice President, Technology
Jason Dole

Director, Human Resources
Bev Ecker

Editorial

Director, Print Publishing
Tom Evans

Managing Editor
Jeff De La Rosa

Editor
William D. Adams

Manager, Contracts & Compliance
(Rights & Permissions)
Loranne K. Shields

Manager, Indexing Services
David Pofelski

Librarian
S. Thomas Richardson

Digital

Director, Digital Product Development
Erika Meller

Digital Product Manager
Jonathan Wills

Manufacturing/Production

Manufacturing Manager
Anne Fritzinger

Proofreader
Nathalie Strassheim

Graphics and Design

Senior Art Director
Tom Evans

Senior Designer
Don Di Sante

Media Editor
Rosalia Bledsoe

Special thanks to:

Roberta Bailey
Nicola Barber
Francis Paola Lea
Claire Munday
Alex Woolf

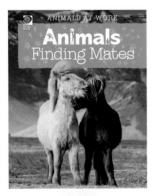

A pair of Icelandic horses during courtship.

Acknowledgments

Cover photo: © Petr Simon, Shutterstock

Alamy: 5 (Malcolm Schuyl), 10-11 (Jukka Palm), 11 (Poelzer Wolfgang), 17 (Adam Fletcher/Biosphoto/Photononstop), 20-21 (Rosanne Tackaberry), 21 (Alex Parrent), 22-23 (David Tipling Photo Library), 23 (Wayne Lynch/All Canada Photos), 25 (Stefan Huwiler/imageBROKER), 26 (Shaun Cunningham), 27 (Avesography), 27 (Christian Ziegler/Minden Pictures), 28-29 (Hturner), 29 (Michael & Patricia Fogden/ Minden Pictures), 31 (Heidi & Hans-Juergen Koch/Minden Pictures), 32 (Jose B Ruiz/ Nature Picture Library), 32-33 (frans lemmens), 33 (Marco Secchi), 36-37 (Jürgen Feuerer), 37 (blickwinkel/Teigler), 39 (NaturaLight), 40-41 (DuncanImages), 42-43 (Green Planet Photography), 43 (edward rowland), 44-45 (Yva Momatiuk & John Eastcott/Minden Pictures), 45 (rod williams). **Shutterstock**: title page & 19 (Bert Klangpremchitt), 6-7 (Rich Carey), 7 (Azovtsev Maksym), 8 (Nicole S Glass), 8-9 (Volodymyr Burdiak), 9 (Keneva Photography), 13 (Rich Carey), 14 (Paul Reeves Photography), 14-15 (LittleDogKorat), 15 (jirisykoracz), 16-17 (Curioso), 20 (Grigorev Mikhail), 30–31 (Kletr), 35 (Luke Shelley), 38-39 (Don Mammoser), 41 (William Cushman).

Contents

Introduction

All animals must reproduce—make more animals like themselves—to pass on their **genes. Reproduction** is the process by which animals create offspring, or young. It ensures the survival of an animal's **species.**

There are a very few animals that reproduce by themselves, without another animal being involved. This is called asexual reproduction. Sponges, for example, are animals that reproduce asexually.

Most animals reproduce sexually, in which two animals come together to produce offspring that share each parent's genetic material. An animal's **mate** is the member of the opposite sex that it joins together, or mates, with to reproduce. Animals that sexually reproduce can only do so with members of their own species. Some animals spend their time alone, only coming together with animals of their own species to mate. Some, such as sharks, often have to travel long distances to find a mate. Other animals, such as baboons, live in groups, so mates are easier to find. But they still need to know when a member of the opposite sex is ready and available to mate.

The urge to mate is extremely strong, sometimes causing an animal to risk its life to do so. But this does not mean that animals are willing to mate with the first candidate they find. Many animals will look for mates that are likely to produce strong, healthy offspring.

Animals have many ways to find mates. They exchange (give and receive) signals with each other, including smells, calls, and visual cues. These signals communicate that they are looking for a mate and are ready to reproduce. This book explores the many ways that animals find and choose a mate.

Mating Rituals

Many species have elaborate **mating rituals.** Some birds sing songs, a few kinds of fish show off to females by vibrating their bodies or flashing their tails, and some spiders give gifts to help the mating process. Other animals decide who mates with whom through contests or fights.

A lion and lioness will mate to reproduce.

The Mating Process

In sexual **reproduction,** a sex cell (a **gamete**) from one member of a **species** joins with the gamete of another. Most of the time, the male transfers his gamete (called a **sperm**) to the female's gamete (called an **egg** cell). Some animal species, such as land snails, are **hermaphrodites** (*hur MAF ruh dyts),* so a single animal is both male and female, but such animals still need to **mate** to reproduce. The successful combining of gametes is called **fertilization.** The **fertilized** egg will grow into a new life, combining the **genes** of both parents.

FERTILIZATION

In most creatures that live in water, fertilization takes place outside the female's body. This is called external fertilization. The female lays her eggs and the male sprays his sperm over them in a process called **spawning.** Some sea creatures, such as coral, simply release their sperm to float through the water to the eggs.

In other animals, fertilization takes place inside the female's body—internal fertilization. The animals come together to mate. Most **reptiles** and birds pass sex cells by rubbing their **cloacas** together. In **mammals,** the male puts a body part called the **penis** into the part of the female's body called the **vagina** to pass on his sperm. Many **invertebrates,** including **insects** and **mollusks,** have sex **organs** like those of mammals.

When animals mate, they use different ways of making sure fertilization happens. Female insects and spiders, for example, often hold the male sperm in their bodies until they are ready to lay their eggs. Some mammals, such as foxes, have penises that hook into the vagina so that the female cannot pull away easily. Other male animals, such as mallard ducks, force themselves on the female to fertilize the eggs.

Human attitudes

People usually associate mating and reproduction in humans with love and affection. For most animals, though, mating is driven only by the need to pass on their genes. By human standards, some animal mating behavior might look cute or affectionate, but far more of it is cruel. Animal mating behaviors are instinctual, meaning an animal was born knowing how to perform them. It cannot act any other way. Such behaviors have allowed its species to survive for generations.

Humans often associate sex with love.

The cloud of particles floating over this coral are sperm cells.

SEXUAL MATURITY

Before an animal can successfully **mate** and reproduce, it must reach a particular size or age. Once this stage is reached, animals' bodies start making the **gametes** needed for **reproduction.** This is called sexual maturity. For animals in which the **fertilized eggs** grow inside the female, her body may change to be able to support them. Sexual maturity happens at different times in different animals. A mouse reaches sexual maturity at six weeks, but a brown bear takes four to eight years.

Some animals, such as **insects** and **amphibians,** go through dramatic body changes before they can reproduce. This process is called metamorphosis (*meht uh MAWR fuh sihs).* A butterfly hatches as a caterpillar, but can only reproduce after it has changed into an adult butterfly. A frog hatches as a tadpole but will only mate as an adult frog.

MATING SEASON

Animals often reproduce in a particular season so the young can grow up in a time with lots of food and good weather. Many birds, which grow quickly, mate in the spring so that they have enough food to give their young. In some larger **mammals,** mating may happen earlier to give the **embryo** time to grow. Deer, for example, mate in the winter so that their young are born in the spring. Some animals are less affected by seasonal change, but females still have particular times when they can **conceive.** For example, female dogs come **in heat** about four times a year.

MATING AGAIN

Some kinds of animals may reproduce several times per season. Others, especially large mammals, may only reproduce once every few years. It may take many months for the embryo to be born, and years before the young is ready to survive on its own.

Dragonflies only reproduce once, then die.

Changing seasons

The Townsend warbler migrates each spring to breed (reproduce) where food is plentiful. In recent years, it has begun to migrate and breed earlier, responding to the warmer weather patterns brought about by **climate change.** But some **zoologists** are concerned that the weather is changing faster than the bird's breeding patterns.

Townsend warblers migrate to breed.

This female bear can only conceive again when her cub is about three years old.

FINDING EACH OTHER

For many animals, one of the challenges of sexual **reproduction** is finding a member of the opposite sex to **mate** with. Chemicals called **hormones** cause the changes in animals' bodies that make them sexually mature. These hormones often trigger signals that are sent out to other members of the **species,** telling them that the animal is ready to mate.

SMELL COMMUNICATION

Hormone changes can trigger smell signals called **pheromones** (*FEHR uh mohnz).* **Insects,** fish, **mammals, reptiles,** and **mollusks** are some of the animals that send these out. The female red-garter snake gives off a powerful pheromone that attracts several males at once, and all try to mate with her. In their active mating attempts, the snakes form what is sometimes called a mating bundle.

SOUND SIGNALS

Animals may use sound to find a mate. The males of many species, such as birds, insects, and frogs, use sound to tell females that they are around. The sounds may also be used to tell potential mates how large or clever they are (see pages 26-29).

Even the females of a few species, such as the tiger, may use sound to signal to mates. Tigers generally live alone in forests. A female comes into season (is able to **conceive)** for only a few days at a time, so she needs to quickly tell males that she is ready to mate. First, she signals her readiness to mate with a special scent in her urine, which she uses to mark her **territory.** Later, she begins to roar regularly. The sound carries through the forest, helping males find her.

Breeding grounds

Many animals find their mates by coming to a particular place at a particular time. American and European eels migrate over huge distances from the coasts of America and Europe to breed in the Sargasso Sea of the North Atlantic. No one knows for sure how the eels find their way.

Eels gather in the Sargasso Sea to breed.

Male red-garter snakes bundle around a female as they try to mate.

Selecting a Mate

It may seem that some animals simply **mate** with the first opposite-sex member of their **species** they find. But many animals do reject some potential mates. On the other hand, others may have to compete with members of the same sex to gain a mate. Together, these actions are called **sexual selection.**

In many species, the female chooses her mate. She looks for a male who will give her healthy offspring that have a good chance of surviving into adulthood. The males of these species will show off their strength and fitness in their mating displays. In species where the male and female raise their young together, a female may also look for signs of parenting skills in the male—for example, the female American goldfinch, a bird, partly bases her choice of mate on his ability to find food. Once in a while, the sex roles are reversed: a male seahorse, for example, carries the **fertilized eggs,** so it chooses the female.

The males of some species compete for females. This can include fighting to decide who is the strongest or has **dominance.** This is the case with elephant seals (see page 40). The winning male then mates with the female or, often, many females.

Sexual selection is good for a species as a whole because it allows the fittest, healthiest animals to reproduce and pass on their **genes.** According to **evolutionary theory,** supported by the scientific community, a living thing that is well adapted to its environment is more likely to survive and reproduce. Sexual selection for such traits as size, bright colors, or complex displays happens because these traits are honest signals of fitness: they cannot usually be faked by an unfit animal. For example, a male bird must be strong, healthy, and well-fed to perform a complex mating display. Weak, sick, or hungry males will simply not have the strength or energy to perform the display well.

A male SEAHORSE fertilizes and carries his mate's eggs inside his body.

Color and Size

When choosing a **mate,** many animals are influenced by physical traits. Bright colors or large size may tell them they have found a good potential mate. Birds, in particular, have **evolved** colorful, visual ways of attracting a mate.

BEAUTIFUL FEATHERS

Many birds are known for their beautiful **plumage** (*PLOO mihg*). Most of the time, the male of the **species** has more colorful feathers than the female. The peacock is probably the best-known example of this: he spreads his amazing tail feathers to attract peahens, whose plumage is dull by comparison. Females seem to base their choice of mate on the color of his feathers, the number of eyespots they contain, and the length of the tail. A strong, healthy male will have a good mix of these traits, and hens will sometimes fight each other to mate with one.

SPRING COLORS

The colorful plumage of some male birds becomes even brighter in the spring, when many bird species enter their mating season. Once again, the brighter plumage shows to the female that her potential mate is fit and healthy. The male American goldfinch's feathers look like the female's in winter, but he grows a brilliant coat of yellow and shiny black feathers in the spring. The males flutter their feathers in flight displays. Bright yellow feathers tell the female that the male has a healthy diet and is good at finding food. The female uses this trait in making her choice, as the two birds will raise their chicks together.

A male American goldfinch has bright yellow feathers in the spring.

Long-tailed widowbirds

The males of these African birds grow extremely long tail feathers during the mating season. But the birds do not fly as well and are more easily caught by **predators,** so why have these long tails evolved? Females choose the male with the longest tail they can find, so this advantage outweighs the risk of getting eaten. Though a male with shorter tail feathers is more likely to survive, he is less likely to mate and pass on his **genes** for shorter tail feathers.

A long-tailed widowbird's tail feathers can be over 1 foot (30 centimeters) long.

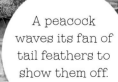

A peacock waves its fan of tail feathers to show them off.

BODY COLORS

Feathers give a bird color, but other parts of their bodies can also be used to attract a **mate.** Some birds have brightly colored feet; others have brightly colored beaks. Atlantic puffins have both. In the winter, puffins' beaks and feet are a dull orange, but in the spring, when the mating season begins, these body parts become much brighter on both sexes. Their beaks also take on a yellow streak. These colors help the birds know the fitness and age of their mate. Puffins often rub their beaks together as part of their **mating ritual.**

SHINY TAILS AND SCALES

Various fish **species** have bright, colorful scales, which often become brighter when they are looking for a mate. **Zoologists** studying the Mexican swordtail fish showed that the females chose the males with shinier tails. A study of guppies found that the females favored males with brighter colors. According to this study, brightly colored males may be better at finding food and also seem more watchful for **predators.**

COLORFUL FACES

Mandrills, a type of large monkey, live in groups, which are led and protected by **dominant** males. Male mandrills have colorful faces with blue cheeks and a red nose. Their rumps are also red and blue. These colors are much brighter in dominant males. Weaker males know this and try not to get into fights with dominant males. Females are attracted to the more brightly colored males, too. For both these reasons, dominant males mate with more females.

Male mandrills have colorful faces.

Peacock spiders

Peacock spiders are so called because of their brightly colored **abdomens.** They show these to the female at the same time as waving their legs. The female spiders usually favor the more colorful males.

A peacock spider displays his colorful abdomen.

A Matter of Size

Many animals consider the size of their potential **mate** in making their choice. A larger animal may be stronger and healthier—traits that they are likely to pass on to their offspring. Male seahorses (see page 12) are attracted to large females for this reason. Size becomes even more important in groups of clownfish.

Clownfish live in small groups in tropical coral reefs, among, or very close to, the stinging tentacles of a sea anemone (*uh NEHM uh nee*). This anemone protects the clownfish, which are immune to its sting, unlike potential **predators.** In return, the clownfish keep the anemone's tentacles clean.

A group of clownfish is usually made up of a mating pair and some smaller, nonbreeding males that join the pair in an anemone. The female of the pair is larger than the **dominant** male. The pair breeds regularly, with the male building a nest close to the anemone for the female to lay her **eggs** in. The breeding male then **fertilizes** the eggs. The smaller males help keep the anemone clean.

If the female dies, though, everything changes. The dominant male grows larger and becomes female. One of the smaller males grows very quickly to take over the position of breeding male. This ability to change sex and grow quickly allows the group to continue to reproduce.

It also leads to a strict order of dominance in the group. The female, as the largest, is at the head of the group, with the adult male next. Both strongly protect their positions. They bite and chase the smaller males, so they are less able to search for food and grow larger. The female wants to make sure that the males do not turn into females, and the dominant male does not want the nonbreeding males to grow and threaten his position. By stopping the smaller fish from growing larger, the mated pair can continue to reproduce.

A female CLOWNFISH is larger than the adult male.

Dances and Displays

Animals may be big, brightly colored, and have all the traits that make them a good choice of **mate.** But they have to let the opposite sex know about these strengths, and they also often face strong competition. As a result, many animals have elaborate **mating rituals** to advertise their fitness to potential mates.

COURTSHIP DANCES

Many mating rituals involve a kind of dancing, where one or both potential mates walk, hop, strut, and perform various body moves in front of the other. These dances may show off particular body parts, such as a bird's feathers or a spider's legs, but they also show that an animal is fit and well. Wandering albatrosses perform complex dances that involve pointing to the sky with their beaks and spreading their wings while facing each other. The birds mate for life, so it is important they choose the right mate. They may engage in such **courtship** for two to three years before they find the right mate. Once they have found their partner, the dances stop.

FLEXIBLE FISH

Guppies reproduce as often as once every four weeks. The females will mate with lots of different males, partly basing their choices on the brightness of a male's colors (see page 16). A male shows off his colors by moving his body in an s-shape, extending and quivering his fins at the same time. Males with the most energetic displays generally mate with more females.

A male guppy quivers his tail fins.

Albatrosses "sky point" in their courtship displays.

Head bobbing

The brown anole lizard is a medium-sized, drab lizard that lives in the Caribbean. Male brown anole lizards have a cool way to attract a mate. The male puffs up a bright orange patch of skin on its throat, called a dewlap, bobs its head up and down, and performs pushups. Researchers have found that the males will do much less head-bobbing when **predators** are around.

A male brown anole lizard shows off his dewlap.

STANDING OUT IN A CROWD

Animals often gather in groups to find and choose a **mate.** These groups are called **leks,** and the male animals that form them are said to be lekking. Lekking males will return to the same places year after year, competing for the attention of females. These competitions are often rowdy, and can sometimes get violent.

Lekking is especially common among birds, including some **species** of grouse, duck, and hummingbird. The males gather on a piece of land or a tree and pick an area of it as their **territory,** which they defend from other males. They also show off to the females by strutting, fluffing up their feathers, spreading their wings, and making different calls. The birds that perform most energetically—and show the most aggressive behavior—usually mate with the most females.

Birds of paradise, from the tropical forests of the island of New Guinea, are famous for the male's beautiful **plumage.** But the bright colors are not enough to attract females on their own. The males gather in leks among the trees to perform complex dances that show off their feathers. They also call out with whistles and clicks. These displays may go on for several hours at a time. The dull-colored females are picky: they inspect each male closely and make their choice based on the quality of both the male's plumage and his display.

LIZARD FIGHTS

Other types of animal also gather in lek-like groups, including **mammals** (such as some seals), fish (such as Atlantic cod), and **insects** (such as swallowtail butterflies). The males of one **reptile,** the marine iguana, gather in leks on the rocky coasts of the Galapagos Islands in the breeding season. They wrestle with each other over territory and the females.

Male bird of paradise displaying at a lek.

Central territory

Sage-grouse gather in leks during the mating season. The males compete for the territory before the females arrive. The males who dominate the group and hold the central area will mate with the most females.

Larger, older sage-grouse win the center ground in their leks.

Displaying Together

Because the choice generally lies with the female in **sexual selection,** often only the male of a **species** displays. In these cases, males and females will usually **mate** several times with different partners to make sure that they successfully reproduce. After mating, the female will usually raise her young alone. But some species are **monogamous** (*muh NOG uh muhs):* they mate only with one partner in a season. Most monogamous pairs also raise their young together, so mating becomes about forming a bond. In these instances, the male and female will often display together.

Many species of bird are known for their amazing joint displays. One of the best known is that of the grebe, a type of freshwater bird. A great crested grebe's **courtship** often begins with the female calling to the male. When the two find each other, they face each other with their necks extended and crests of feathers on the top of the head raised up. Then they shake their heads and raise their wings. The birds may dive and exchange gifts of waterweed. At the high point of the display, the pair rises out of the water together and seems to run across its surface.

A GREAT CRESTED GREBE offers a gift of waterweed to its future mate as part of their mating ritual.

From this display, the birds move on to nest building. They will build several nests together using water plants, creating platforms hidden in the reeds. Again, this seems to be part of the bonding process. When the two are finally satisfied with a nest, they mate and the female lays the **eggs** in it. The pair will take turns to **incubate** the eggs, and then care for the young together when they hatch. They take turns carrying the growing chicks out into the water on their backs. In this way, a partnership that begins with a joint mating display grows into shared parenting that successfully raises the next generation.

Songs and Calls

Sound can be a big part of the way animals find and attract **mates.** It may simply help animals find each other. Or, sometimes, animals use more complex sound signals to make a member of the opposite sex choose them as a mate.

MUSIC MAKERS

Some animals make a kind of music to attract a mate. Birdsong is an example of this. Most birds make calls, but only the males of some bird **species** sing. They do this to mark their **territory** but also to show off to females. Canaries, nightingales, sparrows, and thrushes all sing for these reasons.

LEARNING ABILITY

A song sparrow sings many different short tunes to attract a mate, learning these tunes from other sparrows perched in neighboring branches. Scientists have found out that the greater the number of tunes a sparrow sings and the better he learns them, the more success he has in finding a mate. Researchers think the ability to learn well shows that the bird is healthy and had a good diet when he was young.

OTHER SINGERS

Some species of whale, such as humpback and blue whales, sing songs during their breeding season that travel long distances through the water. Male mice create a type of high-pitched tune to attract their mates. Pairs of **apes** called gibbons sing together as a way of bonding. Song is usually not the only way in which an animal finds a mate. Animals combine singing with other ways of communicating.

Sound and Smell

The male greater sac-winged bat of Central and South America attracts females by flying in front of them, sending a scent toward them from a bodily fluid held in his wing sacs, and performing a trilling song. This song can last anywhere from four minutes to an hour.

The wing sac of the male greater sac-winged bat. It sings and wafts scent from these sacs to attract a female.

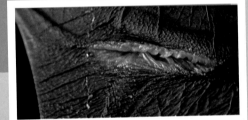

A male song sparrow finds an exposed perch on a branch to sing to attract a mate.

LOUD SOUNDS

There are also other signals a female can pick up from the sounds males make to help her decide which to mate with. Female birds are attracted to males who sing loudly and energetically. A loud singer is a healthy potential **mate.** Louder songs and calls also travel farther, potentially reaching more females.

Fish called cod gather in **spawning** grounds at particular times of year to mate. The males create a noise, sometimes described as grunting, by using muscles that drum on their **swim bladders.** Research has shown that cod with larger drumming muscles have greater mating success, likely because they can make louder sounds.

DEEP CALLS

Large animals can usually make deeper calls. In this way, females can find the largest males in their area by comparing the calls they hear. In Australia, male koalas bellow (roar) to attract females. Their loud grunts continue through the day and night. Each male has his own special call. The larger the koala, the louder and deeper he can bellow. The females pick up on these differences and choose the larger males as mates.

Male alligators bellow all year round. But they bellow more during the mating season. The way the call of a male alligator sounds reveals his size to a female and helps her make her choice. The female will only mate with a male that is larger than she is.

A male koala bellows through the tree tops.

Frog chorus

Tungara frogs of Central America are small but noisy. The males make a two-part sound: first a whining "tung" and then a croaky "gara" to attract a female. Larger males call faster and lower, and, in general, attract more females.

A tungara frog inflates its throat sac to make its two-part call.

Gifts and Tricks

Many animals have ways of **mating** that go beyond making simple sounds and smells. These include giving gifts, offering a home, and even trickery.

FOOD OFFERINGS

As part of his **mating ritual,** a male kingfisher brings fish to a female and feeds it to her, showing her that he is a bird that is good at finding food. It also helps build a bond between the pair when they go on to raise their chicks.

Several **insects,** including butterflies and beetles, give food gifts as part of their **courtship.** The female eats her present while the male mates with her. For example, the male scorpion fly gives the female a blob of his saliva to eat. The saliva is, in fact, very nutritious and helps the female to successfully lay her **eggs.** Male fireflies send **nutrients** along with their **sperm** that may help feed the female as she lays their **fertilized** eggs.

LONG-TERM CAMPAIGN

Chimpanzees are **apes** that live in groups and usually have more than one mate. In one study, scientists watched males regularly raiding a local papaya plantation and giving the fruit they stole to females they wanted to mate with. After a while, the females mated with them. Other studies have shown that female chimps will take food during mating seasons because they have less time to find food themselves. They have to spend their time dealing with males that want to mate with them.

Chimps may share food to attract mates.

Spider strategies

Female spiders are known to eat potential mates. Even if a female allows a male to mate with her, she may eat him during or after mating. In some **species,** males try to avoid this fate by giving the female a silk-wrapped insect to eat as they approach her. On the other hand, the male redback widow spider of Australia flips his **abdomen** over during mating to encourage the female to eat it. He dies, but he makes sure the female he is mating with is well-fed and so will produce healthy offspring.

A male black widow spider approaches the larger female.

NEST BUILDERS

Many animals build some kind of home or nest in which to lay their **eggs** or raise their young. In birds, pairs often do this together during or after their **courtship** as part of the bonding process (see page 25). But among many weavers, the male builds the elaborate nest, showing off the weaving skills that give the birds their name to attract a female. The male displays in front of his nest and the female makes her choice.

A male African village weaver that has failed to attract a **mate** will destroy his rejected nest and build a new one.

A male village weaver constructs his nest.

THREE-SPINED STICKLEBACKS

This fish **species** lives in or close to the open sea but comes into rivers and lakes to breed in fresh water. During this breeding period, the male builds a nest in the water and defends a **territory** around it. He starts by digging a small pit and filling it with weeds and sand. He then swims through the ball-shaped nest to create a tunnel. He now looks for a female, attracting her attention with a zigzag dance into the nest to lay her eggs in the tunnel, which he then **fertilizes.** After this, the male chases the female away. He protects the eggs and guards the young when they first hatch.

Pebble nests

Gentoo penguins of Antarctica build their nests from pebbles, the most common material in the coastal areas where they usually breed. They line the nest with feathers and moss. As part of their courtship, a male penguin will often give his mate a pebble to use in their nest. Sometimes they steal these pebbles from other nests, causing fights to break out.

A gentoo penguin carries a pebble to its nest. The bird may use as many as 1,700 pebbles.

A male stickleback builds his nest.

Bowerbirds

One of the most famous animal builders is the bowerbird, the name given to about 20 **species** of bird found in Australia and neighboring islands. They are named after the amazing structures called bowers the males build as part of their **mating rituals.**

The bowers are not nests but stages where the males will display, singing and dancing, to attract their **mate.** Each species builds a different kind of bower. They start with the same ingredients, twigs and grasses, but from here the variations begin. Some species create arches and tunnels, others U-shaped arenas. The great bowerbird makes an avenue of twigs and attracts the females in by placing objects in the bower in a way that makes them look bigger than they are. An artist would call this forced perspective, but no one knows if the bowerbirds understand their own methods.

Other bowerbirds use more showy decorations, equally happy with natural materials or human garbage. They decorate their bowers with colorful flowers, shiny, sun-bleached bones, strips of plastic, and shards of glass. They place these objects in a way that catches the light or looks nice with other objects in the bower. When a female approaches, the male begins his display.

Bowerbirds that build the most striking bowers, with a strong structure and well-placed decorations, will mate with the most females. Some males will build bowers for several years, improving their skills, before they are chosen as a mate. Females visit different bowers and study them before choosing a mate. By choosing the male with the best bower, a female is betting that her chicks will inherit the health and intelligence of their father—and for the male chicks, his attractive bower-building ability. The female is not looking for any help from her mate, for she will build the nest and raise her chicks on her own.

This SATIN BOWERBIRD has decorated his bower with blue objects.

CRYING WOLF

Some animals will use what people might call trickery to improve their chances of successful **mating.** For example, topi antelope of the African grasslands have a brief mating season, and females are **in heat** for only one day. A female will mate with about four different males several times to make sure that she **conceives.** The more times she mates with a male, the more likely he will be the father of her future offspring. To increase his chances of mating with a female again, a male will snort and stare at pretend **predators,** trying to scare the female into staying in his **territory.**

MIXING CALLS

Some male tungara frogs have found a way of attracting females even if they are smaller (see page 29). They will call beside another frog whose song is slower than theirs. Even if another faster-calling male is in the area, the female seems to prefer the male whose calling speed falls in the middle range.

EMPTY PACKAGES

Some male spiders are known to give the female food wrapped in silk before mating (see page 31). But some males of the *Paratrechalea ornata (pah rah treh KAH lee uh ohr NAH tah)* **species** of South America will trick the female by giving her pieces of grass or even the leftovers of a meal they have already eaten. Because these undesirable gifts are wrapped up, the female may not realize the trick until the male has started mating with her. If a male scorpion fly runs out of saliva to give to a mate (see page 30), he may instead give her a dead **insect.** The male often reuses the same dead insect in future matings.

Male topi antelopes sometimes trick females into staying with them.

Danger tactics

The insects known as water striders or pond skaters have no **mating rituals.** The male simply climbs up on a female on the surface of the water to mate. If the female resists, he drums his legs on the water, attracting fish and insect **predators** below the surface. The female beneath him is most exposed to potential attacks, so she often gives in and allows him to mate, making him stop his life-threatening drumming.

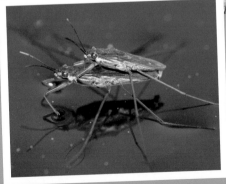

A male water strider mates with a female.

Competing and Fighting

To have a chance to **mate,** males often compete with other males for females. Competition can be intense and aggressive, sometimes leading to fights.

TERRITORIAL DISPUTES

Many males set up a **territory** during the mating season. They will compete for the best area to perform their displays and to attract females. Where large groups gather, competition for the best territory often leads to fights. Male sage-grouse, for example, peck at each other to get the best territory.

The flying dragon, also known as the flying lizard, lives in the trees of southeast Asia. Wing-like structures between its front and back legs allow it to glide up to 200 feet (60 meters) at a time between the branches. Male flying dragons are fiercely territorial. They open their wings to look bigger, and may even chase each other through the air. In this way, the lizards protect their right to mate with the females living in their territory.

TAKING OUT THE OPPOSITION

Great frigatebird males gather in small groups on the islands of the Pacific and Indian Oceans during the mating season. They blow up their bright red throat sacs and call to the females flying overhead. The females choose males with bigger, brighter sacs and join them on the ground. Other males may attack the most successful male in the area, trying to poke a hole in his throat sac. If a male's throat sac has a hole poked in it, he can no longer attract a mate that season, since the sac takes many months to heal.

Ant swarm

Male red harvester ants swarm together in large groups. Their combined **pheromones** attract more females, increasing their chances of mating. But there are still far fewer females than males, so the males fight each other for mates.

Male red harvesters swarm together to attract mates.

A great frigatebird's red throat sac is easy to spot from the air.

WINNER TAKES ALL

A female's choice of **mate** sometimes takes second place to the competition between the males. Some animals, in particular **mammals,** have a system where one **dominant** male mates with a **harem** of females.

Southern elephant seals are the largest of all seals. Males can weigh 8,800 pounds (4,000 kilograms). The females are much smaller— around a fifth of a male's weight. The seals gather in winter and early spring on the shores around Antarctica to mate. The males arrive first and defend a **territory** through threats, roars, and lunges. The largest males fight bloody battles, smashing their chests together to decide which one become a "beachmaster." Their fights continue when the females arrive in a particular territory. A male defends his harem, which may have 40 to 50 females, throughout the mating season so that only he will mate with his females.

MATURE MALES

In harem systems, it is usual for the older males to dominate. An older male gorilla is known as a silverback because of the grey hair he grows on his back. A silverback will lead a troop of gorillas, usually made up of another male, two or three females, and their offspring. Other silverback males will challenge the leader for his females. The dominant male keeps his position by standing on his back legs, beating his chest, and roaring.

Maturing into males

Hogfish are a kind of fish with a long snout. (The snout is the part on the front of an animal's head where the mouth, nose, and jaws are.) Like clownfish (see page 18), the hogfish is a type of **hermaphrodite.** Rooster hogfish live in groups made up of a large male and a harem of several females. The male protects the females from **predators** and aggressively chases away other males. If he dies, a female in the group quickly grows and becomes a male. This allows the group to continue to reproduce.

A rooster hogfish

Male elephant seals fight on a beach.

USING WEAPONS

Some animals have **evolved** body parts that can be used as weapons in the competition for **mates.** Deer, for example, have branched antlers. In most **species,** the males (called stags or bucks) grow new antlers each year. The stags use their antlers during their mating season, called the rut, to compete for **harems** of females. The stags lock antlers, usually without causing serious injury, to decide which is **dominant.** The male with the larger antlers usually wins—their size is a sign of good health—and wins the females that are ready to mate.

Stag beetles are named for the long, antler-like mouthparts that the males grow. The male beetles lock their mouthparts together, wrestling to win control of a suitable spot for females to lay their **eggs,** such as a dead tree trunk. The winning male will then mate with all the females that come to that spot to lay their eggs.

TUSKS

Elephants and walruses are known for their tusks (very long teeth). These can be used as weapons in competition for a mate. Elephant males can become very aggressive when they are ready to mate—a period called musth, after the oily, smelly substance they spray from their **glands** at this time. They will charge each other head-on, clacking tusks, sometimes stabbing their opponent, to win the females. Male walruses also use their tusks when competing for a harem of females.

Sea turtle beaks

A sea turtle has no teeth, but its jaws form a hard, bony beak, which can make an effective weapon. A male will attack another male that is mating with a female, biting him with his beak. He aims to dislodge the mating male from the female's back, hoping to mate with her instead.

Sea turtles have powerful beaks.

Rutting red deer stags fight using their antlers.

Partners for Life

Many birds, such as albatrosses (see page 20), swans, cranes, and penguins, form relationships with a single partner that can last a lifetime. The pairs usually return to the same nesting place from year to year, raising their young together. But there are exceptions to this rule: birds sometimes **mate** with other birds while staying with their partner, or some may find new partners.

FAMILY GROUPS

Some **reptiles** and fish are **monogamous,** as are a few **mammals,** often when in family groups. A pair of wolves that mate for life leads a pack; lar gibbon families center around a lifelong couple. Some small mammals called prairie voles form a lifelong bond after mating, which grows as they raise their young together.

SAME-SEX COUPLES

Many animals, from dolphins to beetles, take part in **homosexual** activity. It is common during the mating season and with animals that have few chances to mate with the opposite sex. Most animals show **bisexual** rather than homosexual behavior, as they will also mate with the opposite sex. These couplings are often linked to social bonding or aiding future **reproduction.**

Some bird **species** form same-sex partnerships that can last a lifetime. Female Laysan albatrosses of Hawaii will pair together, mating with already-paired males to **conceive.** The females nest and raise their young together. This activity allows the birds to reproduce when there are more females than males and still benefit from having two birds to raise their young.

Black swans

Among the black swans of Australia, male pairs are common. To raise a family, one of the males may first mate with a female and chase her away once she lays her **eggs.** Or a pair may steal the nest of a male-female couple. Studies show the males make more successful parents than mixed couples, raising more young to adulthood.

A male black swan guards its nest.

Some prairie voles mate for life.

Glossary

abdomen the rear part of an arthropod's body. An arthropod is an animal with jointed legs and no backbone.

amphibian a vertebrate with scaleless skin that usually lives part of its life in water and part on land. Vertebrate animals have a backbone.

ape a member of a small group of mammals most similar to humans that includes chimpanzees, gorillas, gibbons, and orangutans. Unlike monkeys, apes do not have a tail.

bisexual attracted to both sexes.

climate change a change in the usual weather of a particular place, often associated with global warming.

cloaca a body part of various types of non-mammal animals from which they push out various substances including their feces and, in males, sperm.

conceive create a new life by fertilizing an egg.

courtship the behavior, often repeated, of animals in the lead-up to mating.

dominance, dominant having power or influence over another.

egg a female sex cell, or the structure in which the embryo develops, usually outside the mother's body.

embryo an unborn or unhatched offspring.

evolutionary theory the idea that life has evolved over time, changing to adapt to its environment, and leading to the many different species on Earth today.

evolve in a living thing, to change or develop over the course of many generations.

fertilization when the male gamete (sperm) joins with a female one (egg) to form a new life.

fertilize to join sperm from a male with egg from a female so that a young animal develops.

gamete a sex cell, containing genetic elements of the living thing that has produced it.

gene the unit of inheritance, held in living cells. In most animals, parents' genes are combined in their offspring through sexual reproduction.

gland an organ in an animal's body that secretes (gives off) chemical substances for use in the body or for release into the surroundings.

harem in animals, a group of females controlled by a dominant male.

hermaphrodite an animal with both male and female sex organs, although these may develop at different stages in its life cycle.

homosexual attracted to the same sex.

hormone a chemical produced in a living thing to bring about changes in its cells and body parts.

incubate to keep fertilized eggs warm so that the embryos develop properly and hatch.

in heat the period when certain female mammals are able to conceive.

insect one of the major invertebrate groups. Insects have six legs and a three-part body.

invertebrate an animal without a backbone.

lek a large gathering of male animals who have come together for the purpose of finding mates.

mammal one of the major vertebrate animal groups. Vertebrate animals have a backbone. Mammals feed their offspring on milk produced by the mother, and most have hair or fur.

mate the animal with which another animal partners to reproduce; the act of mating, when two animals come together to reproduce.

mating ritual an action or series of actions, such as dances or calls, that animals perform before mating.

mollusk a class of invertebrates that includes slugs, snails, mussels, and octopuses.

More

monogamous having one mate at a time.

nutrient a substance that is needed to keep a living thing alive and help it grow.

organ a part of the body, made of similar cells and cell tissue, that performs a particular function.

penis the body part through which male mammals urinate and deliver their sperm.

pheromone a chemical substance linked to the sense of smell given out by an animal as a signal to others in its species.

plumage a bird's feathers.

predator an animal that hunts, kills, and eats other animals.

reproduction the process by which living things produce their young, creating the next generation of their species, and passing on their genes.

reptile one of the major vertebrate animal groups. Vertebrate animals have a backbone. A reptile has dry, scaly skin and breathes air. Snakes, crocodiles, and lizards are all reptiles.

sexual selection the natural selection that occurs when one animal chooses, or competes to mate with, another.

spawn to lay and fertilize eggs in water.

species a group of living things that have certain permanent traits in common and are able to reproduce with each other.

sperm a male sex cell.

swim bladder an organ in fish that helps them control the depth they float at in the water.

territory an area of land or water controlled by an animal or group of animals, which they defend from other animals.

vagina the open tube of muscles in female mammals into which a male places his penis to fertilize the eggs held within her body.

zoologist a scientist who studies animals.

BOOKS

The Animal Mating Game by Ann Downer (Twenty-First Century Books, 2016)

Animals and their Mates (Animal Behavior) by Pamela Hickman (Kids Can Press, 2004)

Behavior in Living Things (The Web of Life) by Michael Bright (Raintree, 2012)

Evolution: How All Living Things Came to Be by Daniel Loxton (Kids Can Press, 2010)

Life Processes (The Web of Life) by Anna Clayborne (Raintree, 2012)

WEBSITES

All About Birds
allaboutbirds.org
Created by the Cornell Lab of Ornithology, this website has lots of information about birds, including audio samples of their songs.

BBC Earth
bbc.com/earth/world
BBC Earth has interesting information about earth sciences, including zoology, and astronomy.

National Geographic
nationalgeographic.com
kids.nationalgeographic.com
Find out all sorts of fascinating facts, articles, and videos about animals and how they find mates.

Index